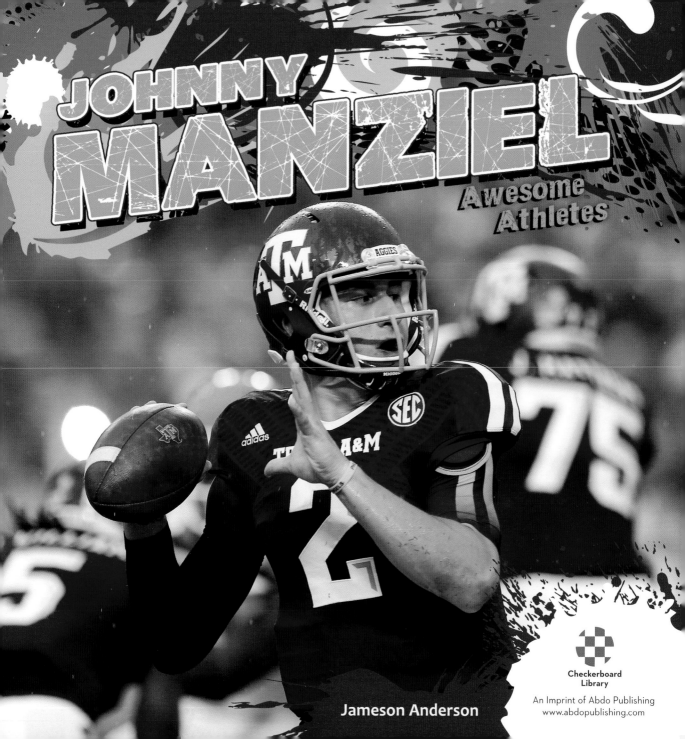

JOHNNY MANZIEL

Awesome Athletes

Jameson Anderson

Checkerboard Library

An Imprint of Abdo Publishing
www.abdopublishing.com

www.abdopublishing.com

Published by Abdo Publishing, a division of ABDO, PO Box 398166, Minneapolis, Minnesota 55439. Copyright © 2015 by Abdo Consulting Group, Inc. International copyrights reserved in all countries. No part of this book may be reproduced in any form without written permission from the publisher. Checkerboard Library™ is a trademark and logo of Abdo Publishing.

Printed in the United States of America, North Mankato, Minnesota.
052014
092014

THIS BOOK CONTAINS
RECYCLED MATERIALS

Cover Photo: AP Images
Interior Photos: Alamy pp. 13, 14; AP Images pp. 1, 5, 7, 9, 11, 17, 19, 21, 23, 25, 26, 27, 29

Series Coordinator: Tamara L. Britton
Editors: Heidi M.D. Elston, Megan M. Gunderson
Art Direction: Neil Klinepier

Library of Congress Cataloging-in-Publication Data
Anderson, Jameson.
 Johnny Manziel / Jameson Anderson.
    pages cm. -- (Awesome athletes)
 Includes index.
 ISBN 978-1-62403-333-9
1. Manziel, Johnny, 1992- 2. Quarterbacks (Football)--United States--Biography--Juvenile litera-
ture. 3. Football players--United States--Biography--Juvenile literature. I. Title.
 GV939.M2895A64 2015
 796.332092--dc23
  [B]
                                    2014010904

TABLE OF CONTENTS

BIG WIN

Before November 10, 2012, not many college football fans outside of Texas had heard of Johnny Manziel. On the campus of Texas A&M, in College Station, he was known as "Johnny Football." To the rest of the country, he was just a first-year starter facing the number-one ranked Alabama Crimson Tide.

Texas A&M was new to college football's Southeastern Conference (SEC). The team, ranked number 15, wasn't expected to compete well right away against powerful teams such as Alabama. But Manziel didn't care what the experts thought. He knew he was a good enough player to lead his team to victory.

That day, a crowd of more than 100,000 people filled Bryant-Denny Stadium in Tuscaloosa, Alabama. Another 10 million watched on TV. Manziel completed 24 of 31 passes for two touchdowns. He passed for 253 yards (231 m) and rushed for another 92 yards (84 m). A&M scored the first 20 points and never looked back.

Manziel led the A&M Aggies to a 29–24 win. Fans around the country wondered if it was just a fluke. Did Alabama have a bad day, or was Johnny Football for real? Could he be a college football superstar? Was he headed to the **National Football League (NFL)**?

Johnny Manziel was A&M's passing leader in the game against Alabama. The win left the Aggies 6–0 on the road and gave them their first victory over a number-one ranked team since 2003.

HIGHLIGHT REEL

Johnathan Paul "Johnny" Manziel was born in Tyler, Texas.

1992

On September 20, Manziel accepted a scholarship to play at Texas A&M.

2010

Manziel led the Aggies to a win over number-one ranked Alabama on November 10.

2012

On May 8, the Cleveland Browns drafted Manziel with the 22nd overall pick.

2014

2010

Manziel broke a state record with 75 passing attempts in a single game.

2011

Manziel graduated from Kerrville Tivy High School early and headed to Texas A&M.

2012

On December 8, Manziel became the first freshman to win the Heisman Trophy.

JOHNNY MANZIEL

DOB: December 6, 1992
Ht: 6'0"
Wt: 210
Position: QB
Number: 2

CAREER STATISTICS:

Passing Yards:	7,820
Passing Touchdowns:	63
Rushing Yards:	2,169
Rushing Touchdowns:	30

AWARDS:

AP Player of the Year Award: 2012
Davey O'Brien Award: 2012
Heisman Memorial Trophy: 2012 (1st), 2013 (5th)
Manning Award: 2012

TYLER, TEXAS

Johnathan Paul "Johnny" Manziel was born in 1992 on his dad's birthday, December 6. He was born in Tyler, Texas. His parents are John Paul, called Paul, and Michelle Manziel. Johnny has a younger sister, Meri.

Johnny's extended family earned money from an oil business in Texas. Johnny's great-grandfather, Bobby Joe, was born in Lebanon. He was a boxer called the "Syrian Kid" before pursuing a career in the oil industry. He struck it rich drilling for oil and settled in Tyler.

Even though Johnny's family was wealthy, his father still worked as a house builder and later a car salesman. Johnny's mother became a real estate agent. The couple met in high school, where they both played golf.

Golf became a family tradition. Johnny's home in Tyler was on the sixteenth hole of Hollytree Country Club. Johnny's first experience with sports was golfing with his family. Johnny and his mother would play against his father and Meri.

Johnny was extremely competitive with his family. When he would lose to his father and sister, he would go to his room upset. He had a hard time accepting that he had lost. He remained focused on winning as he grew up.

Johnny's mother joined him at the 2014 NFL Draft.

YOUTH SPORTS

By the time he was 10 years old, Johnny could compete with adults on the golf course. But Johnny wasn't a one-sport kid. He played basketball, and he **excelled** at baseball. In fact, he was so good that the youth baseball league put an extra net above the outfield fence. Johnny still cleared it for a home run!

Yet in Texas, football is the major sport. Still, Johnny's mother didn't want him to play football in elementary school. She was worried he would get hurt. So, Johnny spent time watching youth teams play.

Johnny's mother let him start playing football in sixth grade. Even with less experience than other kids, Johnny was immediately a star player. The Tyler Hurricanes beat all the other teams in their area. On weekends, Johnny's coaches bused the kids to play more challenging teams around the Dallas area.

By seventh grade, Johnny could throw a football through the high school goal posts from the 50-yard (46-m) line! His natural talent and love of the game would help him eventually reach college and the pros.

A GROWING STAR

When Johnny was in seventh grade, his family moved to Kerrville, Texas. Kerrville is more than five hours away from Tyler, where Johnny was becoming a sports star. Yet Johnny quickly caught the attention of sports fans in his new town.

Johnny played for the Kerrville Tivy High School Fighting Antlers. By sophomore year, he was the **varsity** starting quarterback. That year, Johnny rushed for 835 yards (764 m) with 15 touchdowns. He was 74 for 120 passing for 1,109 yards (1,014 m) and just five **interceptions**. That added another 11 touchdowns.

Johnny's junior season was the fall of 2009. He threw for 2,782 yards (2,544 m) with 19 touchdowns. He rushed for 1,529 yards (1,398 m) with 33 touchdowns.

Johnny was named Most Valuable Player (MVP). In addition, he was named the San Antonio Express-News's

Freshman year, Johnny started playing as a wide receiver. During the fourth game of his sophomore season, he was moved to quarterback. This was the role for which he would become known.

2009 football offensive player of the year. And for the 2009–2010 school year, he was named the Express-News's athlete of the year. Plus, he still had one more season to make his mark.

During the 2010 season, Johnny continued to make a name for himself in Texas high school football. People traveled from all over the state just to see him play.

As a senior, Johnny threw for 45 touchdowns and only five **interceptions**. He completed 228 of 347 passes for 3,609 yards (3,300 m). He also rushed for 1,695 yards (1,550 m) and 30 touchdowns.

For the second year in a row, Johnny was named MVP and offensive player of the year. He was also voted the number one quarterback in Texas high school football by a Texas football magazine.

Even with success on the field, Johnny faced many challenges off the field. Johnny's father, Paul, had made him a deal. Paul knew there was pressure on students to try alcohol. He didn't want Johnny to get in trouble with drinking. So, he offered to buy him a car if he promised not to drink his junior and senior years.

One summer night, Johnny was caught drinking alcohol. The police brought Johnny to jail. The next day, Paul sold the new car he had bought for Johnny. He wanted to make sure Johnny learned from his mistake.

Johnny had to go to court because he was drinking underage. The judge ordered Johnny to do 10 hours of **community service**. Paul didn't think 10 hours was enough. He told the judge to make it 20 hours instead.

MORE THAN FOOTBALL

IN ADDITION TO FOOTBALL, JOHNNY PLAYED BASEBALL IN HIGH SCHOOL. HE WAS AN ALL-DISTRICT SHORTSTOP FOR THE FIGHTING ANTLERS. HE HAD A .416 BATTING AVERAGE.

COLLEGE CHOICE

As Johnny became a high school football star, many colleges became interested in having him play for their teams. Johnny was scheduled to graduate in 2011. So, many coaches were looking to Johnny to lead their teams starting that fall. **Scouts** kept an eye on him.

Johnny received offers from colleges around the country. The University of Oregon, Louisiana Tech, Iowa State, and Stanford were just a few of his options. Johnny and his family decided the University of Oregon, in Eugene, was the best choice.

In June 2010, Johnny spoke to coaches and verbally committed to attend the University of Oregon. Johnny had the rest of the summer, fall, and winter to look forward to playing for Oregon. In the meantime, he had his high school senior season to play!

WHAT MATTERS MOST

JOHNNY HAS SAID HE HAS FOUR PRIORITIES IN LIFE. THEY ARE FAITH, FAMILY, FOOTBALL, AND FRIENDS.

Johnny faced Louisiana Tech on the field on October 13, 2012. A&M won the high-scoring game 59–57. Johnny took top stats for rushing, with 19 carries and 191 yards (175 m) for three touchdowns.

Still, Johnny wished he could play for a college team closer to home. He loved Texas. And, it would be easier for family to see his games. Johnny was about to get his wish.

CLOSE TO HOME

On August 30, 2010, Texas A&M offered Johnny a football **scholarship**. He didn't say yes right away. Johnny attended three games at A&M that fall. He wanted to see what the college football crowds were like. That's when Johnny fell in love with A&M.

On September 20, Johnny officially committed to play at Texas A&M instead of Oregon. He completed his senior year of football. In January 2011, he graduated early and **enrolled** at A&M. He would **major** in sports management.

Johnny's dream of leading a college football team wasn't going to happen as quickly as he thought. The coaches at A&M decided to have him **redshirt** his freshman year. This extended the time he was eligible to play at A&M. However, it was very hard on Johnny. He wanted to play! He finally joined the **roster** in spring 2012.

Johnny still loved baseball. He told both Oregon and A&M he would consider playing for them. Yet football took over immediately. Still, Johnny was drafted by the San Diego Padres in the twenty-eighth round of the 2014 Major League Baseball Draft.

THE COLLEGE FIELD

Manziel's official first season almost didn't happen. On June 29, 2012, Manziel spent time in jail after a fight in College Station. Witnesses said he was trying to break up a fight between a friend and another person. But when police arrived, Manziel gave them a fake ID card.

Somehow, Manziel still proved he could lead the Aggies. On August 15, he was named starting quarterback. His first start was a 20–17 loss to the Florida Gators on September 8. Still, Manziel was A&M's first freshman to start a season-opening game since 1944.

On September 29, Manziel led the Aggies past the Arkansas Razorbacks to a 58–10 win. He set school and SEC records for yards of total offense with 557 (509 m). The record had been held by Archie Manning, father

BOWL GAME RECORD

TEXAS A&M EARNED A TRIP TO THE JANUARY 4, 2013, AT&T COTTON BOWL. THE AGGIES DEFEATED THE OKLAHOMA SOONERS 41–13. MANZIEL HAD FOUR TOUCHDOWNS AND A RECORD 516 TOTAL YARDS (472 M). HE WAS NAMED OFFENSIVE MVP.

of **NFL** stars Peyton and Eli, since 1969! Yet on October 13, Manziel broke the record again with 576 yards (527 m) against Louisiana Tech. In that game, he also had six touchdowns.

Manziel's win over Alabama on November 10 officially put him on the list of hot college quarterbacks. The Aggies ended the season with five straight wins to finish 11–2. Manziel set SEC and **NCAA** records with 5,116 yards (4,678 m) of total offense for the year. He also took first in the SEC with 1,410 rushing yards (1,289 m).

Manziel threw a school-record 453 yards (414 m) for three touchdowns against Arkansas in 2012.

HEISMAN TROPHY

With Manziel posting such great **statistics**, coaches and sports experts started mentioning the Heisman Memorial Trophy. The Heisman is the top award given out in college football each year. It had been awarded 77 times to the best player. But a freshman had never won.

On December 8, 2012, Manziel went to the Best Buy Theater in Times Square in New York City, New York. He was one of three college football finalists to attend the ceremony in which the Heisman Trophy would be awarded.

Manziel received the most first-place votes. He beat out Notre Dame's Manti Te'o and Kansas State's Collin Klein. He was the first freshman ever to win the honor and the first Aggie since 1957.

RECORD BREAKER

IN 2012, MANZIEL RECORDED MORE THAN 5,000 TOTAL YARDS (4,572 M) AND MORE THAN 1,000 RUSHING YARDS (914 M). HE IS THE FIRST NCAA PLAYER TO DO THIS IN JUST ONE SEASON.

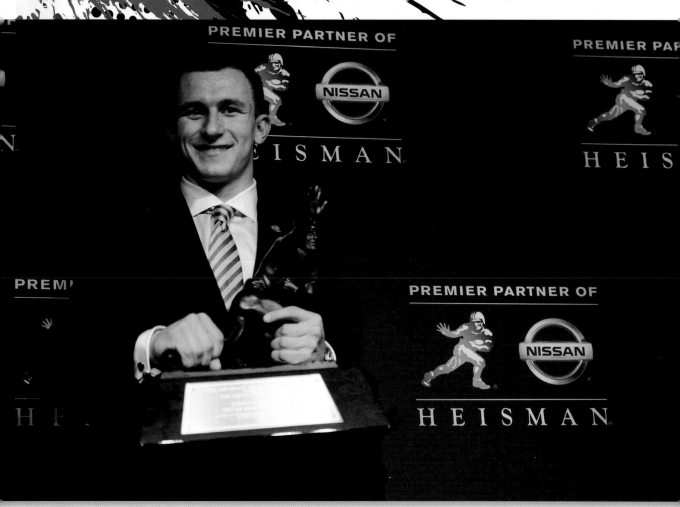

Manziel won the trophy based on the votes of 928 sports journalists and former Heisman winners.

In his acceptance speech, Manziel said he was experiencing a moment he had dreamed of since childhood. Manziel thanked his family and his coaches and celebrated winning the Heisman for all of A&M's players and fans.

SECOND SEASON

What is left after winning college football's ultimate award? Manziel knew that to play in the **NFL**, he needed to have another successful college football season. The Aggies entered the 2013 season ranked seventh. Aside from winning the Heisman, Manziel now also felt the pressure of leading a top-10 team.

Manziel did not have a good start off the field. On August 4, news broke that the **NCAA** was investigating a college football player for illegally selling autographs. College athletes can sign autographs, but they are not allowed to make money from them.

Autograph dealers claimed Manziel was paid for signing thousands of football helmets, photos, and other items. Manziel was not found guilty, but he was suspended for the first half of A&M's season-opening game against Rice University. The Aggies won 52–31. For their second game, they beat Sam Houston State 65–28.

Then, the Aggies faced Alabama. On September 14, all eyes were on Manziel. Could he grab another victory over one of the best college teams in history? Manziel threw for five touchdowns and a career-best 464 yards (424 m). But it wasn't quite enough to get the win. Alabama beat the Aggies in College Station 49–42 in front of more than 87,000 fans.

Manziel was the passing leader with 426 passing yards (390 m) and three touchdowns against Sam Houston.

The 88,504 fans watching A&M defeat Mississippi made up the third-largest Kyle Field crowd in Aggies history.

Manziel continued to showcase his skills throughout the season. On September 28, Manziel faced Arkansas again. He had 320 total yards (293 m), with 253 yards (231 m) in the first half. The Aggies took the win 45–33 in Arkansas.

Manziel matched his five-touchdown record in a 51–41 win over Mississippi State on November 9. He was the passing leader with 446 yards (408 m). This added to his impressive season total. Once again, Manziel ended the season ranked first in the SEC with 4,873 total yards (4,456 m).

On December 31, the Aggies faced the Duke Blue Devils in the Chick-Fil-A Bowl. At the Georgia Dome in Atlanta, A&M held off Duke to win 52–48. Manziel was a star, passing for 382 yards (349 m) and four touchdowns. He rushed for another 73 yards (67 m) and one touchdown. It will be remembered as his final college football performance.

Manziel helped A&M come back for a win after being down 38–17 at halftime against Duke.

THE DRAFT

On January 8, 2014, Manziel announced he was going pro. So, he worked hard to get ready for the 2014 **NFL Draft**. His final college football season was complete, but he continued to work on his skills. He wanted to make sure NFL teams knew he was ready to lead a team at the professional level.

Experts argued how early Manziel would be picked in the NFL Draft. He had impressive college **stats**. He has big hands for a good grip on the ball, and he has an impressive ability to **improvise**. Yet at 6 feet (1 m 83 cm) and 210 pounds (95 kg), he is relatively small. Experts felt his throwing **accuracy** needed improvement, and his problems off the field were a concern.

TRAINING FOR THE PROS

MANZIEL WORKED WITH TRAINER GEORGE WHITFIELD JR. FOR THREE YEARS. WHITFIELD HELPS QUARTERBACKS IMPROVE THEIR GAMES. HE HAS ALSO WORKED WITH NFL QUARTERBACKS BEN ROETHLISBERGER, CAM NEWTON, AND ANDREW LUCK.

On May 8, Manziel attended the **NFL Draft**. The Cleveland Browns made trades to get two first-round picks. They took Manziel with their second pick, making him twenty-second overall. He was the third A&M player and second quarterback drafted. Manziel said he feels Cleveland is where he's supposed to be and promised to bring heart to the game.

Manziel signed a four-year contract with the Browns worth $8.25 million.

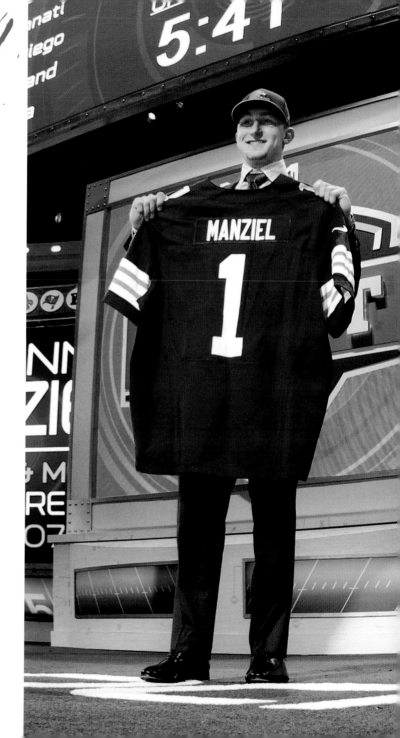

GLOSSARY

accuracy - freedom from error.

community service - unpaid work intended to help society that is assigned to someone who has committed a crime.

draft - an event during which sports teams choose new players. Choosing new players is known as drafting them.

enroll - to register, especially in order to attend school.

excel - to be better than others.

improvise - to make up as you go along, without planning.

interception - a pass thrown by a quarterback that is caught by a player on the opposing team.

major - to study a particular subject or field.

National Football League (NFL) - the highest level of professional football. It is made up of the American Football Conference (AFC) and the National Football Conference (NFC).

NCAA - National Collegiate Athletic Association. The NCAA supports student athletes on and off the field. It creates the rules for fair and safe play.

redshirt - to limit a college athlete's participation in a sport for one school year.

roster - a list of players on a team.

scholarship - money or aid given to help a student continue his or her studies.

scout - a person who evaluates the talent of amateur athletes to determine if they would have success in the pros.

statistics - also called stats. Numbers that represent pieces of information about a game or player. Passing yards, touchdowns, and tackles are a few football statistics.

varsity - the main team that represents a school in athletic or other competition.

To learn more about Awesome Athletes, visit **booklinks.abdopublishing.com**. These links are routinely monitored and updated to provide the most current information available.

INDEX